Every Child Needs Music

Being a music teacher, caring adults often ask me how to help guide the child showing musical aptitude, or when to begin music lessons. My reply depends on the resources available, followed by "Start as soon as possible." The benefits of music reach far beyond learning how to sing or play an instrument. Belonging to an organized music group enhances a child's success in society, success in school, and success in life. Caring parents value these positive benefits, but the recent studies regarding mental development impact their parental decisions. The studies show that music training *profoundly* affects brain development.

With advancements in technology, including PET and MRI scans, researchers literally watch and chart brain activity while a person engages in various tasks. Researchers quickly discovered that music is one of the very few whole brain functions, engaging all four parts of the brain! The *only* other activities that use both hemispheres are higher-level mathematics and logic processing, such as chess. All other tasks rely on the dominant use of either the left or right brain. Furthermore, the research shows the brain's ability to continue to develop with proper stimulation and exercise. **Nothing compares to music education in brain stimulation and development.** The plethora of music and brain research articles makes it clear—music education benefits *every* child.

Why does engaging in music activate the entire brain? A musician's mind is constantly choosing how fast or slow to play, with what style, rhythm, phrasing, and feeling—training the brain to become incredibly good at organizing while simultaneously controlling finger movement, reading and memorizing. Thus, a musician conducts numerous mental and physical activities at the same time—training the brain to organize and create multiple mental pathways.

These mental skills and multiple mental pathways, honed by music education, permeate *all* facets of learning, and the effects continue to compound over time with advanced music study. One example of the effects publicized in 2001, a Profile of SAT Program Test Takers, reported students participating in music scored higher on the SATs than students with no arts participation. Scores for students in music performance classes were 57 points higher (Verbal) and 41 points higher (Math). Scores for students in music appreciation classes were 63 points higher (Verbal) and 44 points higher (Math).* It is no coincidence that a high percentage of band, choir, or orchestra members are top-ranking students.

What better way to develop a child's mind than consistent engagement in musical activities? There is no better way. *Regardless* of a child's natural tendencies for the arts, making music instruction a part of every child's total development can only enhance his or her life skills and mental processing.

Every child deserves the multiple benefits of music education.

I developed Freddie the Frog products to provide an accessible and entertaining form of music education for use at home. I encourage you to enjoy Freddie's adventures and to pursue other music education opportunities available in your area. (More suggestions listed in the back of the book.)

Further information on the benefits of music education at: *www.musicfriends.org/benefits.html* **or** *www.supportmusic.com*.

Sharon Burch

* College-Bound Seniors National Report: Profile of SAT Program Test Takers. Princeton, NJ: The College Entrance Examination Board, 2001

FREDDIE THE FROG® AND
THE BASS CLEF MONSTER

Written by **Sharon Burch**

Illustrated by **Tiffany Harris**

· 2ND ADVENTURE: BASS CLEF MONSTER ·

MYSTIC PUBLISHING, INC. · Mystic, Iowa

To my dad and mom, Byron and Felva Tait—I am forever grateful for your example of love, wisdom and integrity; forever humbled by the witness you live; and forever honored to be your daughter. I love you more than I have ever been or will ever be able to express. Thanks for being the best parents either Byranna or I could have ever had.
—*S.B.*

To Hal and Lyn Marie Wood—my finest teachers, true encouragers, and wise guides.
—*T.H.*

Text © 2006 by Sharon Burch
Illustrations © 2006 by Tiffany Harris

Printed in China by Jade Productions.   03/11
Book design and production by **The Kids at Our House**
The artwork in **Freddie the Frog® and the Bass Clef Monster** rendered in watercolor pencils and acrylic on black and white drawing paper.

The soundtrack on the audio CD accompanying **Freddie the Frog® and the Bass Clef Monster** was composed and performed by Grant Wood and Jonathan White with the exception of public domain music, "Ah! Vous Dirais-je, Maman."

Narration and character voices by Jonathan White.
Bass Clef Monster character voice by Bruce Watley.
Lady Elephant and Bee character voices by Tiffany Harris.

Publisher's Cataloging-in-Publication
Provided by Quality Books, Inc.

Burch, Sharon (Sharon Kay)

Freddie the frog and the bass clef monster / written by Sharon Burch; illustrated by Tiffany Harris.
p. cm. + 1 sound disc (digital; 4 3/4 in.). —(2nd adventure. Bass clef monster)
SUMMARY: Freddie the frog introduces readers to the bass clef, which serves as a pictorial outline of his scary dream during hibernation.
Audience: Ages 4-9.
Includes compact disc.
LCCN 2005929330
ISBN-13: 978-0-9747454-8-0
ISBN-10: 0-9747454-8-0

1. Frogs—Juvenile fiction. 2. Music—Juvenile fiction. [1. Frogs—Fiction. 2. Music—Fiction.]
I. Harris, Tiffany. II. Title. III. Title: Bass clef monster

PZ7.B91586Bas 2006   [E]
QBI05-600094

10 9 8 7 6 5 4 3 2

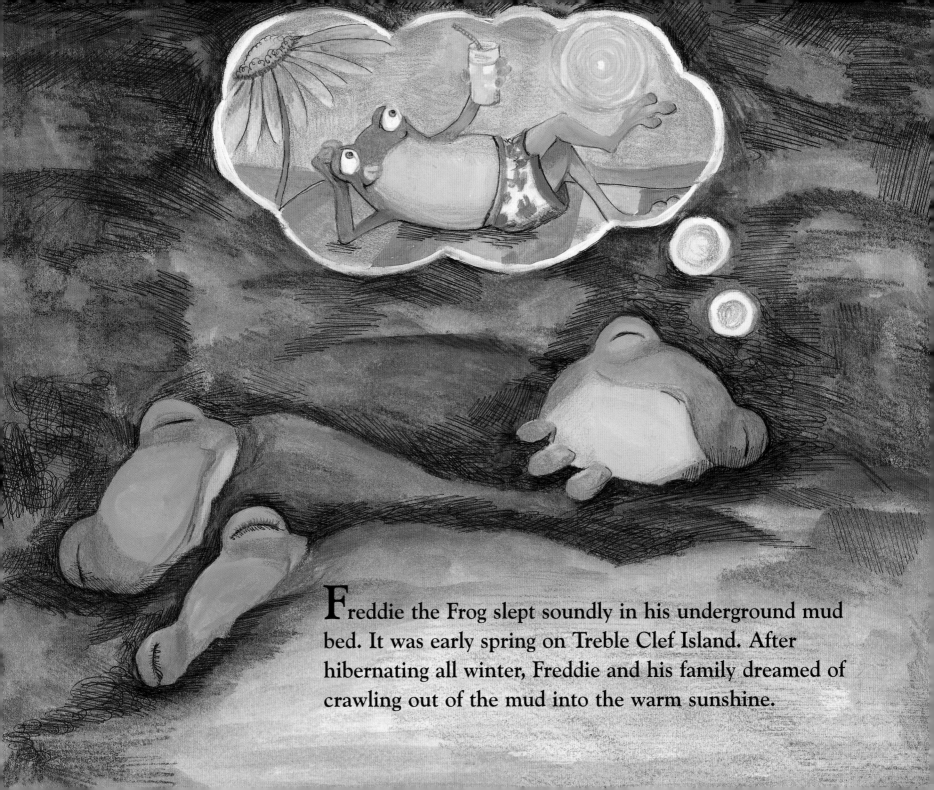

Freddie the Frog slept soundly in his underground mud bed. It was early spring on Treble Clef Island. After hibernating all winter, Freddie and his family dreamed of crawling out of the mud into the warm sunshine.

As the mud grew warmer, the sleeping Freddie wriggled to the surface.
Freddie could not wait to play with his elephant friend, Eli. Freddie
opened his groggy eyes and wondered, "Where am I?"
This did not look like Treble Clef Island.

Freddie cautiously hopped in and peered through the darkness.

Slam! Freddie jumped as the gate closed behind him.

Freddie found himself standing in the middle of an orchard of...

Any smart frog knows that where
apple trees grow, tasty flies swarm!
After the long hibernation,
Freddie was hungry.

"Slurp, slurp, slurp."
Freddie gobbled flies as fast as
his tongue could move.

When he had eaten as much as his bulging belly would hold, he decided to explore and search for Treble Clef Island.

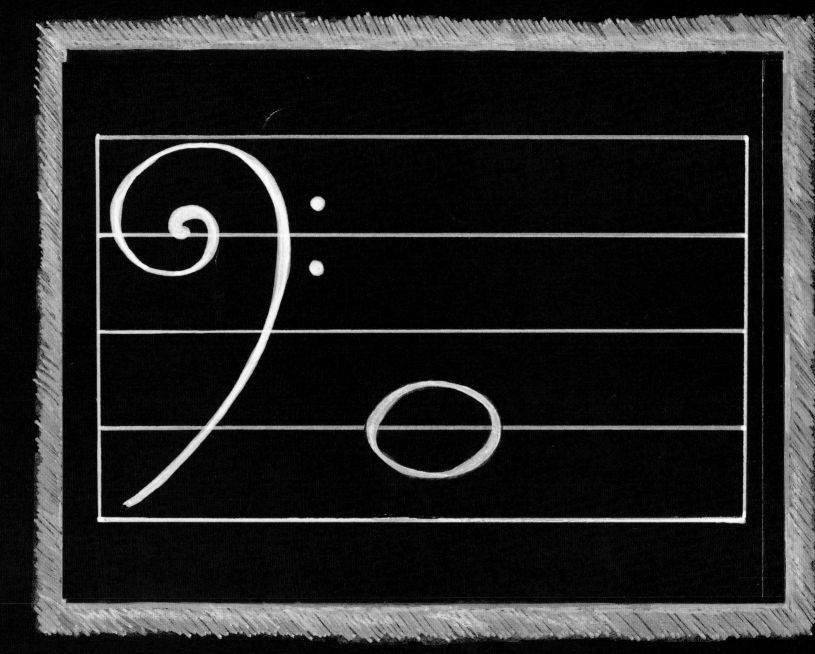

Freddie remembered his aching, swollen tongue of last summer. (He made the mistake of slurping a bee instead of a fly!) Then one bee spotted Freddie and flew straight at him.

"Greetingszz, Froggie!" buzzed the bee.
"Iszz there zomething I can do for you?"

"I'm looking for Treble Clef
Island," said Freddie warily. "Do you
know where it is?"

"Bzzz....No, but the Bass Clef
Monster *loveszz* frogszz. Why don't
you ask him?"

Then the wall of bees separated to make a path for Freddie. The bees even pointed him on his way. Freddie gingerly hopped backwards as he kept his eyes on them.

Freddie's eyes bulged. Cocoons covered the ground—cocoons as big as Freddie—and some were wiggling!

Freddie cautiously tiptoed past
the eerie shapes.

Phew! Freddie sighed with relief as he passed the last strange cocoon. But he relaxed too soon.

The fierce dragon looked down its long
scaly nose at Freddie and smiled smugly.
    "Oh, you're a frog. I'm sorry.
How can I help you, little frog?"
the dragon rumbled, blowing smoke
rings at Freddie.
    "I-I-I'm looking for Treble
Clef Island. D-D-Do you know
how to get there?" Freddie choked.

"No, but the Bass Clef Monster *loves* frogs.
Why don't you ask him?" drawled the dragon. And he
slowly turned and lumbered to his den.

Freddie journeyed on in search of the Bass Clef Monster. He hoped the monster could help him find his way home.

Soon, even though the sky was still murky, he spied something large and gray in the distance. The Bass Clef Monster?

"Eli!" Freddie exclaimed as he quickly hopped to meet his friend.

"Get off my foot, you little…oh, frog. So sorry," said the strange elephant, peering over her glasses at Freddie. "How can I help you, little frog?"
"I-I-I'm looking for Treble Clef Island. Do you know how to get there?" Freddie inquired nervously.
"No, but the Bass Clef Monster *loves* frogs. Why don't you ask him?" said the elephant.

Before Freddie could reply, the elephant plopped Freddie on top of her wrinkled head.

"I will take you myself," she said, tromping down a well-worn path. They came to a long bumpy log, and the elephant carefully placed Freddie on top of it.

"Now, little frog, wait right here. This is the…

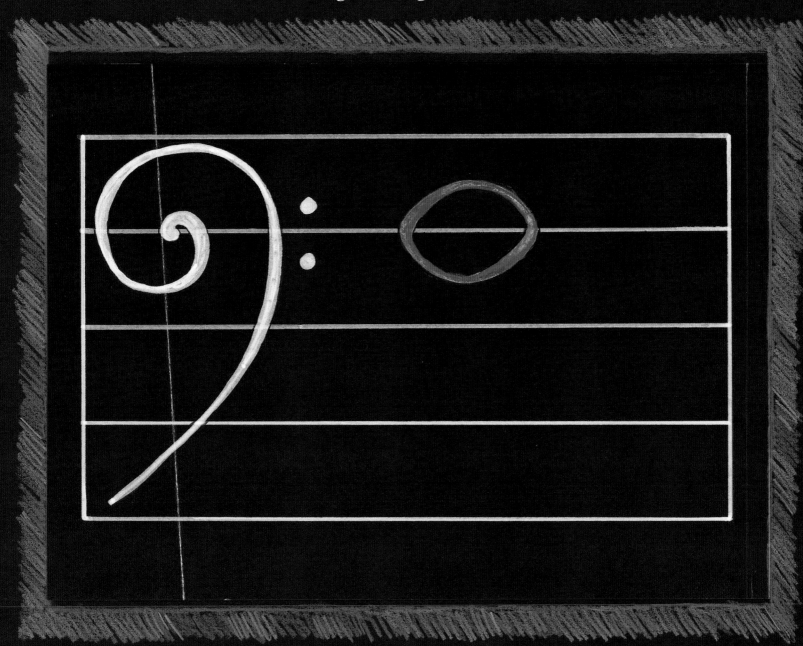

Freddie waited nervously. The wind blew stronger. It began to howl. Freddie's insides quivered.

"Something is not right," Freddie thought, trembling. He was scared!

Freddie could not sit on that Frog Log any longer. He sprung into the tall...

Terrified, Freddie quaked so hard the grass around him shook and rattled.
"Hey! Hey, you! Stop shaking the grass! I can't hold on!" yelled a tiny voice.

Surprised, Freddie stopped. He looked at the far side of the patch of grass.
"Who said that?" Freddie squeaked.

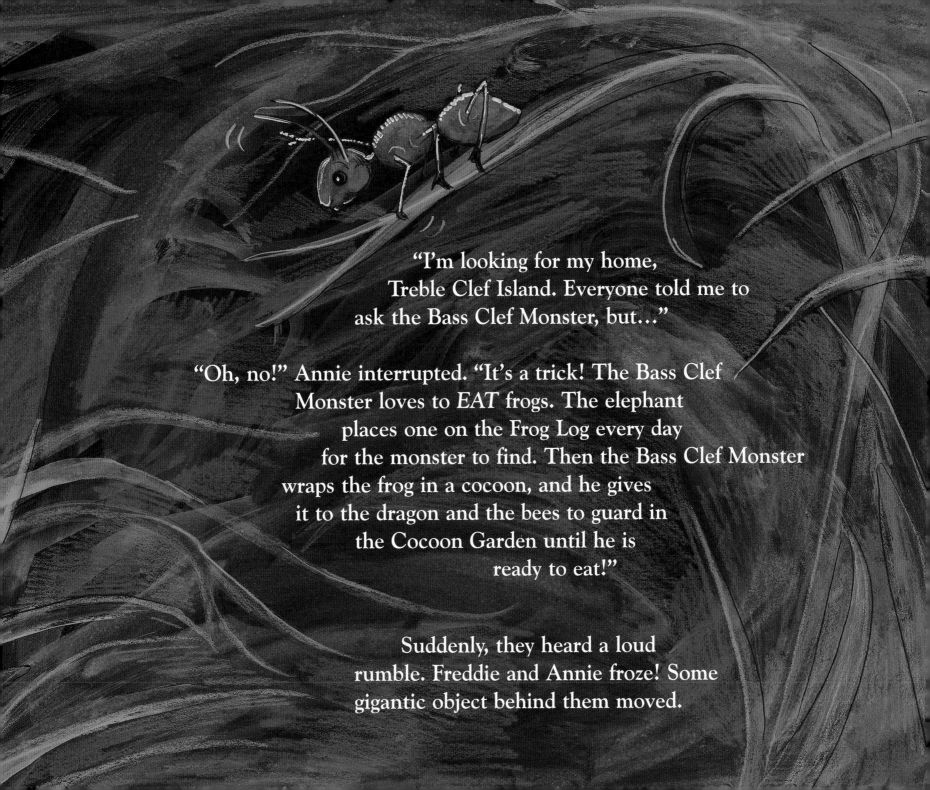

"I'm looking for my home,
Treble Clef Island. Everyone told me to
ask the Bass Clef Monster, but…"

"Oh, no!" Annie interrupted. "It's a trick! The Bass Clef
Monster loves to *EAT* frogs. The elephant
places one on the Frog Log every day
for the monster to find. Then the Bass Clef Monster
wraps the frog in a cocoon, and he gives
it to the dragon and the bees to guard in
the Cocoon Garden until he is
ready to eat!"

Suddenly, they heard a loud
rumble. Freddie and Annie froze! Some
gigantic object behind them moved.

"Ha, ha, ha!" roared the monster as he snatched Freddie out of the grass. "Thought you could hide from me did you, little frog? Well, not anymore. Ha, ha, ha!" The monster spewed white fiber out of his mouth. He wound it around and around the little frog!

"Ahhhhh!" screamed Freddie as he fought to escape. *"Ahhhhh!*
Don't eat me!
Don't eat me!
*Don't eat me! **Ahhhh!"***

"Hold still, you little *frog*!
You can't escape me now!"
But Freddie struggled even harder. It was no use.
"Help! Help! Let me out! Let me out!" Freddie screamed.
The Bass Clef Monster encased him in a cocoon. Freddie
struggled frantically. He opened his eyes wide,
but he could not see anything.

Suddenly, Freddie felt something grab him and pull him out of the cocoon. It lifted him up into green grass and blue skies. He felt sunshine on his face and found himself in the middle of a great big hug.

"Mom! Dad! Eli! I'm home! I'm back home! Oh, what a horrible dream!"

Freddie hopped for joy to see his best friend, Eli, waiting for him.
The nightmare quickly vanished in the warm spring breeze.

Now Freddie's real adventures were about to begin—on Treble Clef Island!

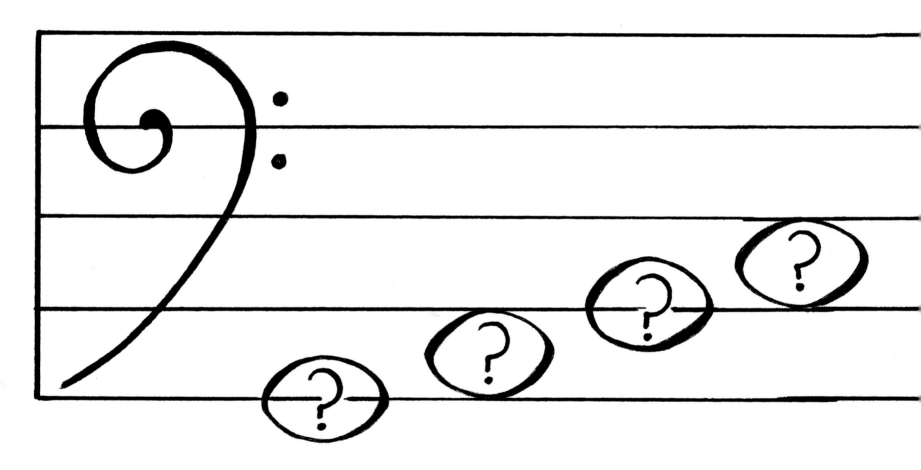

Do you remember what or who is at each place on the staff?

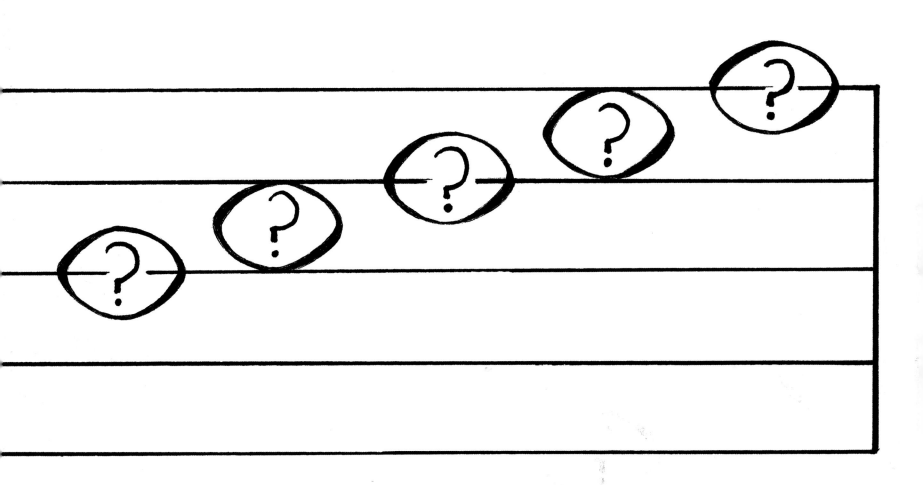

FREDDIE the FROG® BOOKS

Freddie the Frog® and the Thump in the Night
1st Adventure: Treble Clef Island
Book/CD

Discover the magic of Freddie the Frog® (and learn music too!)

Freddie the Frog® and the Secret of Crater Island
4th Adventure: Crater Island
Book/CD

Freddie the Frog® and the Bass Clef Monster
2st Adventure: Bass Clef Monster
Book/CD

Freddie the Frog® and the Mysterious Wahooooo
3rd Adventure: Treble Clef Island
Book/CD

Thump in the Night
Flashcard Set 1

Bass Clef Monster
Flashcard Set 2

Freddie the Frog®
Hand Puppet

Mysterious Wahooooo
Magnetic Rhythm Set

Crater Island
Flashcard Set 3

Treble Clef Island
Poster

Bass Clef Monster
Poster

MYSTIC PUBLISHING, INC.
BRADLEY BANK BLDG., 2ND FLOOR • 307 N. 13TH • CENTERVILLE, IA 52544
1-800-596-5448   FAX 641-856-6046